Fresh Fat-Quarter Quilts

12 Projects for Your Favorite Fabrics

• • • • • • • • • • • •

• • • • • • • • • • • •

Andy Knowlton

Martingale®
Create with Confidence

Fresh Fat-Quarter Quilts: 12 Projects for Your Favorite Fabrics
© 2019 by Andy Knowlton

Martingale®
19021 120th Ave. NE, Ste. 102
Bothell, WA 98011-9511 USA
ShopMartingale.com

Printed in China
24 23 22 21 20 19   8 7 6 5 4 3 2 1

Library of Congress Control Number: 2019941844

ISBN: 978-1-68356-035-7

MISSION STATEMENT

We empower makers who use fabric and yarn to make life more enjoyable.

CREDITS

PUBLISHER AND
CHIEF VISIONARY OFFICER
Jennifer Erbe Keltner

CONTENT DIRECTOR Karen Costello Soltys	DESIGN MANAGER Adrienne Smitke
MANAGING EDITOR Tina Cook	PRODUCTION MANAGER Regina Girard
ACQUISITIONS AND DEVELOPMENT EDITOR Laurie Baker	COVER AND BOOK DESIGNER Mia Mar
TECHNICAL EDITOR Carolyn Beam	PHOTOGRAPHER Brent Kane
COPY EDITOR Melissa Bryan	ILLUSTRATOR Sandy Loi

SPECIAL THANKS
Photography for this book was taken at:
Blackberry Hill Farm in Carnation, Washington
The home of Julie Thomas in Maltby, Washington
The home of JoAn Reynolds in Snohomish, Washington

Contents

Introduction

One of my favorite ways to purchase fabric is to buy fat quarters. When my kids were young I often had them with me when I went to the quilt shop. Out of necessity I had to shop quickly–little boys aren't patient in quilt shops and the less time spent there, the less of a mess they can make. Knowing that I had to be quick, I would head to the display of fat quarters, grab what I needed, and be on my way. No waiting in line at the cutting table!

In a quilt shop you can find fat quarters sold individually or prepackaged, either in bundles from the manufacturer or in custom bundles curated by the shop–and those are the fun ones! While bundles are definitely convenient, it's also fun to start from scratch and create your own. Don't be afraid to mix and match individual fat quarters to suit your own style.

Not only are fat quarters convenient, but they're also versatile. They can be cut into strips for strip piecing, used for appliqué, and usually there are enough repeats of a design in a fat quarter to make it perfect for fussy cutting. Also, if you're working with directional fabric or a large-scale print, a fat quarter gives you more versatility than a ¼-yard cut would, because you'll get 18" of width.

I've often heard quilters proclaim their love for a fat-quarter bundle but in their next breath say that either they don't know what to make with it, or they're saving it for the "perfect" pattern. This book is meant to inspire you to open those packs and create with them. As pretty as a bundle of fabric is, it's even prettier in a finished, usable quilt!

The quilts in this book are grouped according to the number of fat quarters needed, either 6, 8, 10, 12, or 14. So grab a stack of fat quarters you love, and then open the book to see what you can make.

~ *Andy Knowlton*

Lucky Star

fat quarters
6

The Sawtooth Star block is a classic, and I love any variation of it. This version, with the on-point square in the center, also goes by the name Mosaic. Whatever you call it, four fun Star blocks made from just six fat quarters let you start and finish your quilt in a flash. Try using a contrasting fabric for the star points to really make them pop.

materials

Yardage is based on 42"-wide fabric. Fat quarters measure 18" × 21".

- 1 fat quarter of yellow print for block centers
- 1 fat quarter of green print for block centers
- 4 fat quarters of assorted aqua prints for blocks
- 1⅛ yards of white dot for background, sashing, and border
- ⅞ yard of white solid for star points
- ½ yard of green print for binding
- 3⅛ yards of fabric for backing
- 52" × 52" piece of batting

finished quilt: 45½" × 45½"
finished block: 18" × 18"

cutting

All measurements include ¼" seam allowances.

From the yellow print fat quarter, cut:

3 strips, 5½" × 21"; crosscut into 8 squares, 5½" × 5½"

From the green print fat quarter, cut:

3 strips, 5½" × 21"; crosscut into 8 squares, 5½" × 5½"

From *each* of the 4 aqua print fat quarters, cut:

1 strip, 9½" × 21"; crosscut into 4 rectangles, 5" × 9½" (16 total)

1 strip, 5½" × 21"; crosscut into 2 squares, 5½" × 5½" (8 total)

From the white dot, cut:

2 strips, 5½" × 42"; crosscut into 8 squares, 5½" × 5½"

7 strips, 3½" × 42"; crosscut *1* of the strips into 2 strips, 3½" × 18½"

From the white solid, cut:

5 strips, 5" × 42"; crosscut into 32 squares, 5" × 5"

From the green print yardage, cut:

5 strips, 2½" × 42"

making the blocks

Press the seam allowances as indicated by the arrows.

1. Draw a diagonal line from corner to corner on the wrong side of each yellow 5½" square.

2. Place a marked yellow square on a green 5½" square, right sides together. Sew ¼" from each side of the drawn line. Cut along the drawn line to make two half-square-triangle units. Trim the half-square-triangle units to measure 5" square, including seam allowances. Make 16 units.

  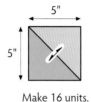

Make 16 units.

3. Arrange four units in two rows of two with the green print in the center as shown. Join the units in each row, and then join the rows to make a square-in-a-square unit that measures 9½" square, including seam allowances. Repeat to make four square-in-a-square units *total*, two with green centers and two with yellow centers.

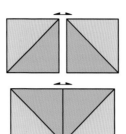 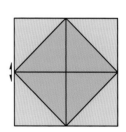

Make 2 units,
9½" × 9½".

Make 2 units,
9½" × 9½".

4. Referring to steps 1 and 2, make 16 half-square-triangle units using the white dot and aqua squares. Trim each half-square-triangle unit to 5" square, including seam allowances.

  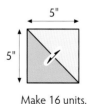

Make 16 units.

7. Arrange four half-square-triangle units, a square-in-a-square unit, and four star-point units in three rows. Sew the units together into rows, and then join the rows to complete a Sawtooth Star block that measures 18½" square, including seam allowances. Make four blocks.

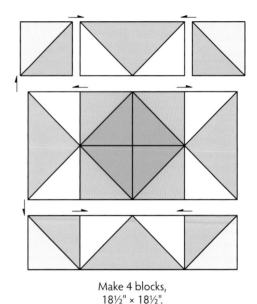

Make 4 blocks,
18½" × 18½".

assembling the quilt top

1. Referring to the quilt assembly diagram on page 11, arrange the Sawtooth Star blocks in two rows of two, adding a white dot 3½" × 18½" sashing strip between each pair of blocks.

2. Sew the blocks and sashing strips together to make two rows that each measure 18½" × 39½", including seam allowances. Trim one white dot 3½"-wide strip to 39½" long and join the rows to this center sashing strip. The quilt center should measure 39½" square, including seam allowances.

3. Cut two of the white dot 3½"-wide strips to 39½" long. Sew these strips to opposite sides of the quilt top.

5. Draw a diagonal line from corner to corner on the wrong side of each white solid 5" square.

6. Place a marked white square on one end of an aqua rectangle, right sides together and with the line oriented as shown. Sew directly on the drawn line. Trim ¼" from the line and flip the corner open and press. Repeat to sew a marked white square to the other end of the aqua rectangle as shown to complete one star-point unit. Make 16 units that measure 5" × 9½", including seam allowances.

 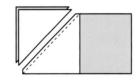
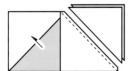 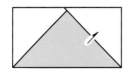

Make 16 units,
5" × 9½".

4. Sew the three remaining white dot 3½"-wide strips together end to end to make one long strip. Press the seam allowances open. Cut two strips, 3½" × 45½", and sew these strips to the top and bottom of the quilt top. The quilt top should measure 45½" square.

finishing the quilt

For more details about any of the finishing steps, go to ShopMartingale.com/HowtoQuilt.

1. Layer the backing, batting, and quilt top; baste the layers together.

2. Quilt by hand or machine. The quilt shown is machine quilted with a diagonal grid of squares within squares.

3. Trim the excess batting and backing fabric from the quilt. Use the green 2½"-wide strips to make double-fold binding, and then attach the binding to the quilt.

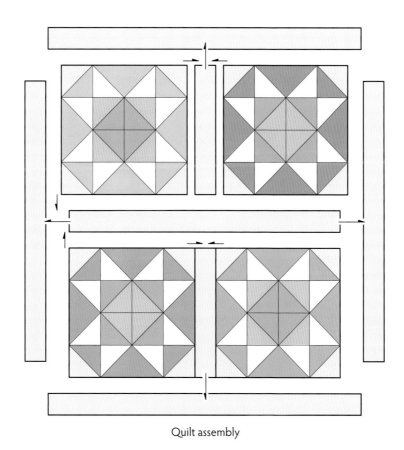

Quilt assembly

Cut Glass

fat quarters
6

Inspiration can be found anywhere. Cut Glass was inspired by a tile pattern I spotted right under my feet one day. The Hourglass blocks in the quilt create a fun secondary design. Choosing a gray fabric with some visual texture adds interest to the quilt without drawing attention away from the main prints.

materials

Yardage is based on 42"-wide fabric. Fat quarters measure 18" × 21".

- 6 fat quarters of assorted prints for Nine Patch blocks
- 3⅛ yards of white solid for background and border units
- 1⅝ yards of gray print for Hourglass blocks and border units
- ⅝ yard of navy print for binding
- 3⅔ yards of fabric for backing
- 66" × 77" piece of batting

finished quilt: 57½" × 68½"
finished block: 5½" × 5½"

cutting

All measurements include ¼" seam allowances.

From *each* of the 6 print fat quarters, cut:

5 strips, 2¾" × 21" (30 total)

1 strip, 1½" × 15" (6 total)

From the white solid, cut:

6 strips, 2¾" × 42"; crosscut into 12 strips, 2¾" × 15"

8 strips, 1½" × 42"; crosscut into 15 strips, 1½" × 21"

5 strips, 7" × 42"; crosscut into 25 squares, 7" × 7"

9 strips, 4¼" × 42"; crosscut into:
- 48 squares, 4¼" × 4¼"
- 18 rectangles, 4¼" × 6"

From the gray print, cut:

5 strips, 7" × 42"; crosscut into 25 squares, 7" × 7"

4 strips, 4¼" × 42"; crosscut into 22 rectangles, 4¼" × 6"

From the navy print, cut:

7 strips, 2½" × 42"

Tips for Accurate Strip Piecing

Strip piecing can be a real time-saver. Instead of cutting and sewing a lot of smaller pieces, you'll sew longer strips together and then cut them into the needed segments. These tips can help improve accuracy when you're strip piecing:

- Check your seam allowance and keep it at a consistent scant ¼" as you sew along the length of the strip.

- Shorten your stitch length slightly to make the stitches more secure since you'll be cutting small segments.

- When sewing more than two strips together, alternate the sewing direction for each strip. After sewing the first two strips together, start stitching the third strip from the opposite end. This will help reduce warping in the final strip set.

- Press carefully. Any pulling or stretching can create a wave or a slight curve in the strip set. Pressing seam allowances to one side will help seams to nest easily in later steps.

- When cutting strip sets into smaller segments, work slowly, measure carefully, and cut just one at a time. It's tempting to stack a couple of strip sets together and cut them all at once, but they will tend to shift because of the long horizontal seams.

making the uneven nine patch blocks

Press the seam allowances as indicated by the arrows.

1. Sew different color or print 2¾" × 21" strips to opposite sides of a white 1½" × 21" strip to make a strip set. Repeat to make 15 strip sets. Crosscut each strip set into 2¾"-wide segments for a total of 100 segments that measure 2¾" × 6", including seam allowances.

Make 15 strip sets, 6" × 21".
Cut 100 segments, 2¾" × 6".

2. Sew white 2¾" × 15" strips to opposite sides of a print 1½" × 15" strip to make a strip set. Repeat to make six strip sets. Crosscut each strip set into 1½"-wide segments for a total of 50 segments that measure 1½" × 6", including seam allowances.

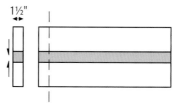

Make 6 strip sets, 6" × 15".
Cut 50 segments, 1½" × 6".

3. Arrange two segments from step 1 and one segment from step 2 in three rows as shown; sew the segments together to make a block. Repeat to make 50 blocks that measure 6" square, including seam allowances.

Make 50 blocks,
6" × 6".

making the hourglass blocks

1. Draw a diagonal line from corner to corner on the wrong side of each white 7" square. Place a marked white square on a gray 7" square, right sides together. Sew ¼" from both sides of the drawn line. Cut along the drawn line to make two half-square-triangle units. Make 50 half-square-triangle units that measure 6⅝" × 6⅝", including seam allowances.

Make 50 units, 6⅝" × 6⅝".

2. Draw a diagonal line from corner to corner on the wrong side of a unit from step 1, perpendicular to the seamline. Place this unit on top of a second unit, right sides together, with the gray prints on opposite sides and the seams nested. Sew ¼" from each side of the drawn line. Cut along the drawn line to make two Hourglass blocks. Trim the blocks to measure 6" square, including seam allowances. Repeat to make 49 Hourglass blocks; you will have 1 extra block.

Make 49 blocks.

3. Draw a diagonal line from corner to corner on the wrong side of each white 4¼" square. Place a marked white square on one end of a gray 4¼" × 6" rectangle, right sides together and with the line oriented as shown. Sew on the drawn line. Trim ¼" from the line and flip the corner up. Repeat to sew a marked white square to the other end of the gray rectangle as shown to make a flying-geese unit. Make 22 flying-geese units that measure 4¼" × 6", including seam allowances.

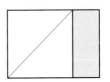 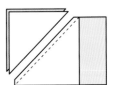

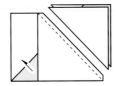 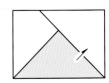

Make 22 units, 4¼" × 6".

assembling the quilt top

1. Arrange five flying-geese units, four white 4¼" × 6" rectangles, and two of the remaining white 4¼" squares as shown. Sew together into a row. Repeat to make two rows that measure 4¼" × 57½", including seam allowances. These will be the top and bottom rows of the quilt.

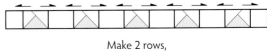

Make 2 rows, 4¼" × 57½".

2. Arrange two flying-geese units, five print blocks, and four Hourglass blocks as shown, noting the orientation of the Hourglass blocks. Sew together to make row A. Repeat to make six A rows that measure 6" × 57½", including seam allowances.

Row A. Make 6 rows, 6" × 57½".

3. Arrange two white 4¼" × 6" rectangles, four print blocks, and five Hourglass blocks as shown. Notice that the Hourglass blocks are oriented in the opposite direction from their placement in the A rows. Sew together to make row B. Repeat to make five B rows that measure 6" × 57½", including seam allowances.

Row B.
Make 5 rows, 6" × 57½".

4. Lay out the A and B rows in alternating positions. Place the flying-geese rows at the top and bottom as shown in the quilt assembly diagram below. Sew the rows together. The completed quilt top should measure 57½" × 68½".

finishing the quilt

For more details about any of the finishing steps, go to ShopMartingale.com/HowtoQuilt.

1. Layer the backing, batting, and quilt top; baste the layers together.

2. Quilt by hand or machine. The quilt shown is machine quilted in an allover design of squares and circles.

3. Trim the excess batting and backing fabric from the quilt. Use the navy 2½"-wide strips to make double-fold binding, and then attach the binding to the quilt.

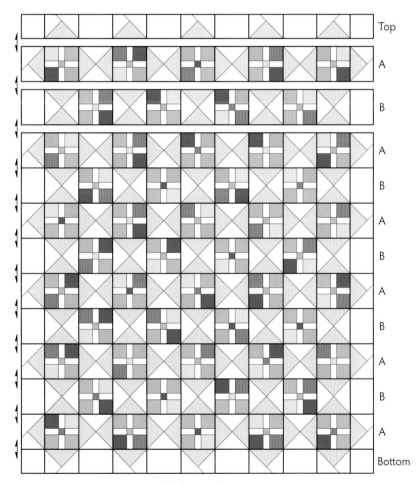

Quilt assembly

Sweet Wishes

Pinwheels and patchwork were meant to go together. In this quilt, the pinwheels share the spotlight and form the centers of sweet flower blocks.

materials

Yardage is based on 42"-wide fabric. Fat quarters measure 18" × 21".

- 8 fat quarters of assorted prints for blocks and pieced borders
- 2⅝ yards of white solid for background, sashing, and outer border
- ½ yard of green print for binding
- 3⅜ yards of fabric for backing
- 59" × 75" piece of batting

So Many Choices

If mixing prints from different fabric companies and designers feels overwhelming, try selecting prints from different fabric lines by a single designer. The prints in this quilt came from five different fabric lines that were all designed by Lori Holt for Riley Blake Designs. They all work together, but the result is a bit scrappier than if I'd selected fabrics from a single collection.

cutting

All measurements include ¼" seam allowances.

From *each* of the print fat quarters, cut:

1 strip, 3¼" × 21"; crosscut into:
  - 4 squares, 3¼" × 3¼" (32 total)
  - 2 squares, 2½" × 2½" (16 total)

2 strips, 2½" × 21"; crosscut into 16 squares, 2½" × 2½" (128 total)

2 strips, 3½" × 21"; crosscut into 16 rectangles, 2½" × 3½" (128 total)

From the white solid, cut:

3 strips, 3¼" × 42"; crosscut into 32 squares, 3¼" × 3¼"

15 strips, 1½" x 42"; crosscut into:
  - 32 rectangles, 1½" × 4½"
  - 32 rectangles, 1½" × 6½"
  - 128 squares, 1½" × 1½"

20 strips, 2½" × 42"; crosscut 8 of the strips into:
  - 64 squares, 2½" × 2½"
  - 12 rectangles, 2½" × 10½"

From the green print, cut:

6 strips, 2½" × 42"

finished quilt: 50½" × 66½"
finished block: 10" × 10"

making the blocks

Press the seam allowances as indicated by the arrows.

1. Draw a diagonal line from corner to corner on the wrong side of each white 3¼" square.

2. Place a marked white square on a print 3¼" square, right sides together. Sew ¼" from each side of the drawn line. Cut along the drawn line to make two half-square-triangle units. Trim the units to measure 2½" square, including seam allowances. Make 64 units.

Make 64 units.

3. To make a pinwheel, arrange four matching half-square-triangle units in two rows as shown. Join the units in each row, and then join the rows to make a pinwheel that measures 4½" square, including seam allowances. Repeat to make 16 pinwheels.

Make 16 pinwheels, 4½" × 4½".

4. Sew white 1½" × 4½" rectangles to opposite sides of a pinwheel. Then sew white 1½" × 6½" rectangles to the top and bottom of the pinwheel. The block should measure 6½" square, including seam allowances. Repeat to make 16 Pinwheel blocks.

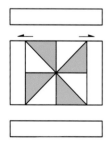 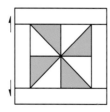

Make 16 Pinwheel blocks, 6½" × 6½".

5. Draw a diagonal line from corner to corner on the wrong side of each white 1½" square.

6. For one block, choose eight matching print 2½" × 3½" rectangles. Place a marked white square on the top-right corner of a print rectangle, right sides together and with the line oriented as shown. Sew on the drawn line. Trim ¼" from the line and flip the corner open. Make four units. In the same manner, make four units with the white square sewn to the top-left corner. The units should measure 2½" × 3½", including seam allowances.

Make 4 of each unit, 2½" × 3½".

Trimming Tip

My favorite tool for trimming half-square triangles is the Triangle Square Up Ruler from Quilt in a Day. With just two quick swipes of my rotary cutter, my blocks are squared up and ready for sewing!

To help reduce bulky seams at the center of the Pinwheel blocks, I recommend taking the time to trim those little dog-ears from the corners before pressing the half-square-triangle units open. The ruler is available in multiple sizes, but I recommend the 9½" size. It can trim all half- and quarter-square triangles from 1" to 9½". So handy!

7. Sew two units from step 6 together as shown. Repeat to make four matching petal units that measure 2½" × 6½", including seam allowances.

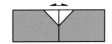

Make 4 units,
2½" × 6½".

8. Arrange one Pinwheel block, four petal units from step 7, and four white 2½" squares in three rows. Sew the units together in rows, and then join the rows to complete a Pinwheel Flower block that measures 10½" square, including seam allowances. Make 16 blocks.

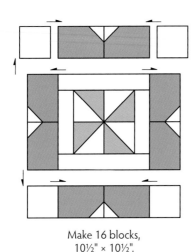

Make 16 blocks,
10½" × 10½".

assembling the quilt top

1. Sew the white 2½"-wide strips together end to end to make one long strip. Press the seam allowances open. From this long strip, cut five 46½"-long strips, two 62½"-long strips, and two 50½"-long strips for the horizontal sashing and outer borders.

2. Referring to the quilt assembly diagram on page 23, arrange the Pinwheel Flower blocks in four rows of four blocks each, positioning white 2½" × 10½" sashing rectangles between the blocks. Add the white 2½" × 46½" sashing strips between the rows.

3. Sew the blocks and sashing rectangles into rows, and then join the rows with the 46½"-long horizontal sashing.

4. To make the patchwork borders, sew the print 2½" squares into six rows of 23 squares each. There are six extra squares, allowing flexibility of color placement within the strips. Each row should measure 2½" × 46½", including seam allowances. Sew the rows together in groups of three to make two border strips measuring 6½" × 46½", including seam allowances.

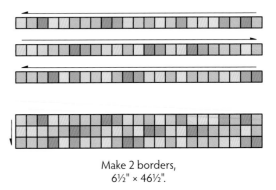

Make 2 borders,
6½" × 46½".

Check Your Seams

Because each patchwork border has a large number of seams, even a tiny variation in the seam allowance will affect the final length of the border strips. Test your seam allowance by sewing two print 2½" squares together. Press the seam and measure the unit. It should be 4½" wide. Adjust the seam allowance if needed, and then continue sewing the rows together.

5. Sew the patchwork borders to the top and bottom of the quilt top.

6. Sew the white 62½"-long border strips to opposite sides of the quilt top. Sew the white 50½"-long border strips to the top and bottom of the quilt top. The completed quilt top should measure 50½" × 66½".

finishing the quilt

For more details about any of the finishing steps, go to ShopMartingale.com/HowtoQuilt.

1. Layer the backing, batting, and quilt top; baste the layers together.

2. Quilt by hand or machine. The quilt shown is machine quilted with an allover feather design.

3. Trim the excess batting and backing fabric from the quilt. Use the green 2½"-wide strips to make double-fold binding, and then attach the binding to the quilt.

Quilt assembly

Perfect Picnic

When my kids were little, one of our favorite summertime activities was to drive to a park in the canyon for a picnic and then spend the afternoon playing at the base of the nearby waterfall. It was the perfect way to spend a hot afternoon.

materials

Yardage is based on 42"-wide fabric. Fat quarters measure 18" × 21".

- 8 fat quarters for blocks and pieced quilt-center border (blue floral, green dot, red plaid, dark yellow print, green plaid, light yellow print, red floral, and light blue print)
- 4½ yards of navy solid for background, sashing, and inner and outer borders
- ½ yard of blue floral for middle border
- ⅝ yard of green print for binding
- 4½ yards of fabric for backing
- 80" × 80" piece of batting

cutting

All measurements include ¼" seam allowances.

From *each* of the blue floral, green dot, red plaid, and dark yellow print fat quarters, cut:

2 strips, 4" × 21"; crosscut into:
- 8 squares, 4" × 4" (32 total)
- 2 squares, 1½" × 1½" (8 total)

2 strips, 3½" × 21"; crosscut into:
- 16 rectangles, 2" × 3½" (64 total)
- 4 rectangles, 2" × 3¼" (16 total)

From *each* of the green plaid and light yellow print fat quarters, cut:

1 strip, 4" × 21"; crosscut into:
- 4 squares, 4" × 4" (8 total)
- 1 square, 1½" × 1½" (2 total)

1 strip, 3¾" × 21"; crosscut into:
- 1 square, 3¾" × 3¾" (2 total)
- 8 rectangles, 2" × 3½" (16 total)

1 strip, 2" × 21"; crosscut into 4 rectangles 2" × 3¼" (8 total)

Continued on page 27

finished quilt: 71½" × 71½"
finished block: 13" × 13"

Continued from page 25

From the red floral fat quarter, see the illustration at right to cut:

2 strips, 5½" × 21"; crosscut into:

- 4 squares, 5½" × 5½"
- 2 squares, 4" × 4"
- 2 rectangles, 2" × 3½"
- 2 rectangles, 2" × 3¼"
- 1 square, 2" × 2"
- 1 square, 1½" × 1½"

1 strip, 4" × 21"; crosscut into:

- 2 squares, 4" × 4"
- 6 rectangles, 2" × 3½"

From the light blue fat quarter, cut:

2 strips, 2¾" × 21"; crosscut into
8 rectangles, 2¾" × 5"

1 strip, 3½" × 21"; crosscut into:

- 8 rectangles, 2" × 3½"
- 2 rectangles, 2" × 3¼"

1 strip, 4" × 21"; crosscut into:

- 4 squares, 4" × 4"
- 1 square, 1½" × 1½"

From the navy solid, cut:

16 strips, 2" × 42"; crosscut into:

- 2 strips, 2" × 23"
- 2 strips, 2" × 20"
- 4 rectangles, 2" × 9½"
- 96 rectangles, 2" × 3½"
- 32 rectangles, 2" × 3¼"

6 strips, 4" × 42"; crosscut into:

- 48 squares, 4" × 4"
- 2 squares, 3¾" × 3¾"

2 strips, 6½" × 42"; crosscut into
48 rectangles, 1½" × 6½"

1 strip, 5½" × 42"; crosscut into 4 squares,
5½" × 5½"

1 strip, 5" × 42"; crosscut into 8 rectangles,
2¾" × 5"

1 strip, 13½" × 42"; crosscut into
12 strips, 2½" × 13½"

10 strips, 2½" × 42"

8 strips, 3½" × 42"

From the blue floral yardage, cut:

7 strips, 2" × 42"

From the green print, cut:

8 strips, 2½" × 42"

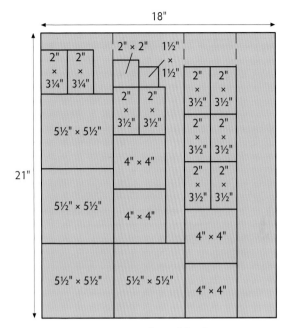

Cutting for red floral

making the large center block

Press the seam allowances as indicated by the arrows.

1. Draw a diagonal line from corner to corner on the wrong side of each red floral 5½" square.

2. Place a marked red square on a navy 5½" square, right sides together. Sew ¼" from each side of the drawn line. Cut along the drawn line to make two half-square-triangle units. Trim the units to measure 5" square, including seam allowances. Make eight units.

Make 8 units.

3. Sew a navy 2¾" × 5" rectangle to a light blue 2¾" × 5" rectangle to make a unit that measures 5" square, including seam allowances. Make eight units.

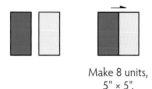

Make 8 units,
5" × 5".

4. Arrange two half-square-triangle units and two units from step 3 into two rows of two. Sew the units together into rows, and then join the rows. Make four corner units that measure 9½" square, including seam allowances.

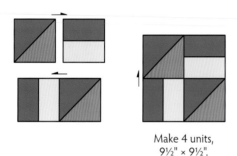

Make 4 units,
9½" × 9½".

5. Arrange the four corner units, the four navy 2" × 9½" rectangles, and the red floral 2" square in three rows as shown. Sew the pieces together into rows, and then join the rows to complete a block that measures 20" square, including seam allowances.

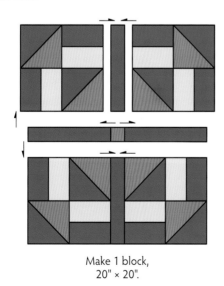

Make 1 block,
20" × 20".

6. Sew the two navy 2" × 20" rectangles to opposite sides of the center block. Then sew the two navy 2" × 23" rectangles to the top and bottom of the center block. The center block will measure 23" × 23", including seam allowances.

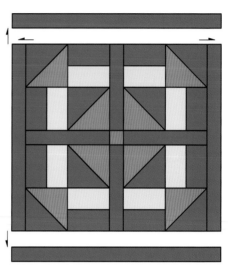

Center block.
Make 1 block, 23" × 23".

adding the quilt-center borders

1. Draw a diagonal line from corner to corner on the wrong side of the light yellow and green plaid 3¾" squares.

2. Place the marked yellow square on a navy 3¾" square, right sides together. Sew ¼" from each side of the drawn line. Cut along the drawn line to make two half-square-triangle units. Trim the units to measure 3¼" square, including seam allowances. Repeat with the marked green square to make a total of four units.

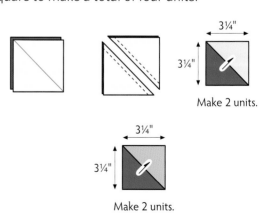

3¼"

3¼"

Make 2 units.

3¼"

3¼"

Make 2 units.

3. Sew eight navy 2" × 3¼" rectangles and seven assorted print 2" × 3¼" rectangles together as shown, starting and ending with a navy rectangle. Make two rows measuring 3¼" × 23", including seam allowances. These will be the side pieced borders.

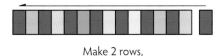

Make 2 rows,
3¼" × 23".

4. Sew one yellow/navy unit, one green/navy unit, eight navy 2" × 3¼" rectangles, and seven assorted print 2" × 3¼" rectangles together as shown. Note the direction of the seams in the half-square-triangle units. Make two rows measuring 3¼" × 28½", including seam allowances. These will be the top and bottom pieced borders.

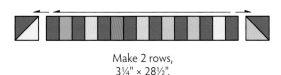

Make 2 rows,
3¼" × 28½".

5. Sew the two side borders to the large center block. Add the top and bottom borders to complete the center block unit. The center block unit will measure 28½" × 28½", including seam allowances.

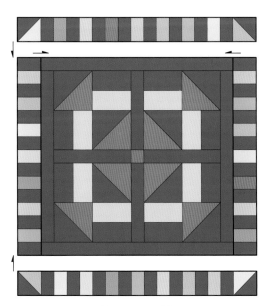

Center assembly

6. Sew the 10 navy 2½" × 42" strips together end to end to make one long strip. Press the seam allowances open. Cut two strips, 2½" × 28½", and sew them to opposite sides of the center block unit. Cut two strips, 2½" × 32½", and sew them to the top and bottom of the center block unit. The quilt center should measure 32½" square, including seam allowances.

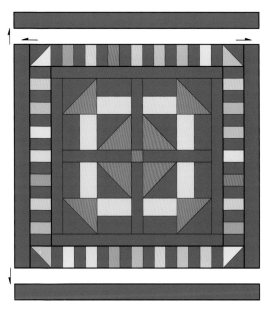

Center section.
Make 1 section,
32½" × 32½".

making the small blocks

1. Draw a diagonal line from corner to corner on the wrong side of four blue floral 4" squares.

2. Place a marked blue square on a navy 4" square. Sew ¼" from each side of the drawn line. Cut along the drawn line to make two half-square-triangle units. Trim the units to measure 3½" square, including seam allowances. Make eight units.

3½"

3½"

Make 8 units.

13½" square, including seam allowances. Make 12 blocks, referring to the quilt photo on page 26 for suggested fabric combinations.

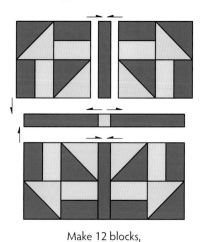

Make 12 blocks,
13½" × 13½".

3. Sew a navy 2" × 3½" rectangle to a dark yellow 2" × 3½" rectangle to make a unit that measures 3½" square, including seam allowances. Make eight units.

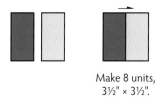

Make 8 units,
3½" × 3½".

4. Arrange two half-square-triangle units and two units from step 3 into two rows of two. Sew the units together into rows, and then join the rows to make a corner unit that measures 6½" square, including seam allowances. Make four corner units.

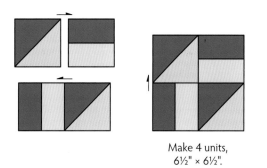

Make 4 units,
6½" × 6½".

5. Arrange the four corner units, four navy 1½" × 6½" rectangles, and a blue floral 1½" square into three rows as shown. Sew the pieces together into rows, and then join the rows to complete a block measuring

assembling the quilt top

1. Sew two small quilt blocks and three navy 2½" × 13½" strips together as shown to make a side unit. Make two side units that measure 13½" × 32½", including seam allowances. Sew the side units to opposite sides of the center section.

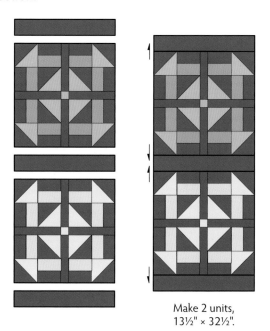

Make 2 units,
13½" × 32½".

2. Sew four small quilt blocks and three navy 2½" × 13½" strips together. Sew this row to the top of the quilt center. Sew the remaining small quilt blocks and three navy 2½" × 13½" strips together. Sew this row to the bottom of the quilt center. The quilt center should measure 58½" square, including seam allowances.

3. From the remainder of the pieced navy strip from step 6 on page 29, cut two strips, 2½" × 58½", and sew them to opposite sides of the quilt top. Cut two strips, 2½" × 62½", and sew them to the top and bottom of the quilt top.

4. Sew the blue floral 2" × 42" strips together end to end to make one long strip. Press the seam allowances open. Cut two strips, 2" × 62½", and sew them to opposite sides of the quilt top. Cut two strips, 2" × 65½", and sew them to the top and bottom of the quilt top.

5. Sew the navy 3½" × 42" strips together end to end to make one long strip. Press the seam allowances open. Cut two strips, 3½" × 65½", and sew them to opposite sides of the quilt top.

Cut two strips, 3½" × 71½", and sew them to the top and bottom of the quilt top. The completed quilt top should measure 71½" square.

finishing the quilt

For more details about any of the finishing steps, go to ShopMartingale.com/HowtoQuilt.

1. Layer the backing, batting, and quilt top; baste the layers together.

2. Quilt by hand or machine. The quilt shown is machine quilted with an allover orange peel design.

3. Trim the excess batting and backing fabric from the quilt. Use the green 2½"-wide strips to make double-fold binding, and then attach the binding to the quilt.

Quilt assembly

Penelope

fat quarters 10

You'll want a fair amount of contrast between the pink and the red prints used in the Sister's Choice blocks to make the design stand out. Swapping out the teal prints for greens would give this quilt a fun Christmas vibe.

materials

Yardage is based on 42"-wide fabric. Fat quarters measure 18" × 21".

- 3 fat quarters of assorted pink prints for Star blocks
- 3 fat quarters of assorted red prints for Star blocks
- 4 fat quarters of assorted teal prints for Chain blocks
- 3½ yards of white solid for background and inner border
- ⅜ yard of medium teal print for middle border
- ¾ yard of light teal print for outer border
- ⅝ yard of dark teal print for binding
- 5⅜ yards of fabric for backing
- 70" × 90" piece of batting

finished quilt: 61½" × 81½"
finished block: 10" × 10"

cutting

All measurements include ¼" seam allowances.

From *each* of the 3 red and 3 pink fat quarters, cut:
5 strips, 2½" × 21"; crosscut into:
- 12 rectangles, 2½" × 4½" (72 total)
- 15 squares, 2½" × 2½" (90 total)

1 strip, 3" × 21"; crosscut into 6 squares, 3" × 3" (36 total)

From *each* of the 4 teal fat quarters, cut:
5 strips, 2½" × 21" (20 total)

From the white solid, cut:
35 strips, 2½" × 42"; crosscut into:
- 20 strips, 2½" × 21"
- 17 rectangles, 2½" × 10½"
- 34 rectangles, 2½" × 4½"
- 216 squares, 2½" × 2½"

3 strips, 3" × 42"; crosscut into 36 squares, 3" × 3"

7 strips, 2" × 42"

From the medium teal print, cut:
7 strips, 1½" × 42"

From the light teal print, cut:
7 strips, 3½" × 42"

From the dark teal print, cut:
8 strips, 2½" × 42"

Mix It Up

Each block is made from two prints, one for the star points and one for the inner star. To ensure a nice variety of blocks throughout the quilt, it pays to take a minute in the beginning and plan out your blocks. Each print will be used as the star points in three blocks and the inner star in three blocks.

making the sister's choice blocks

Press the seam allowances as indicated by the arrows.

1. For one block, choose the following pieces from the same red print: two 3" squares, four 2½" × 4½" rectangles, and one 2½" square. Also select four matching pink 2½" squares.

2. Draw a diagonal line from corner to corner on the wrong side of two white 3" squares. Place a marked white square on a red 3" square, right sides together. Sew ¼" from each side of the drawn line. Cut along the drawn line to make two half-square-triangle units. Trim the units to measure 2½" square, including seam allowances. Make four.

Make 4 units.

3. Sew a white 2½" square to one side of a half-square-triangle unit, noting the direction of the seamline of the unit. Make four units that measure 2½" × 4½", including seam allowances.

Make 4 units,
2½" × 4½".

4. Draw a diagonal line from corner to corner on the wrong side of four white 2½" squares. Place a marked white square on one end of a red 2½" × 4½" rectangle, right sides together and with the line oriented as shown. Sew on the drawn line. Trim ¼" from the line and flip the corner open. Make four units that measure 2½" × 4½", including seam allowances.

Make 4 units,
2½" × 4½".

5. Sew a unit from step 3 to a unit from step 4 to make a unit A. Repeat to make four units that measure 4½" square, including seam allowances.

Unit A.
Make 4 units,
4½" × 4½".

6. Sew a pink 2½" square to a white 2½" square to make one unit B. Repeat to make four units that measure 2½" × 4½", including seam allowances.

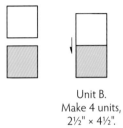

Unit B.
Make 4 units,
2½" × 4½".

7. Arrange four A units, four B units, and one matching red 2½" square into three rows. Sew the pieces into rows; join the rows to complete a Sister's Choice block measuring 10½" square, including seam allowances. Make 18 blocks, half with red star points and pink inner stars and half with pink star points and red inner stars.

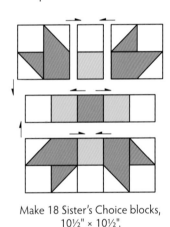

Make 18 Sister's Choice blocks,
10½" × 10½".

making the chain blocks

1. Sew a white 2½" × 21" strip and a teal 2½" × 21" strip together to make a strip set. Repeat to make 20 strip sets. Cut each strip set into 2½"-wide segments for a total of 136 segments that measure 2½" × 4½", including seam allowances.

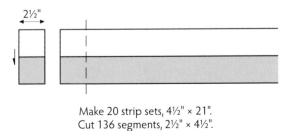

Make 20 strip sets, 4½" × 21".
Cut 136 segments, 2½" × 4½".

2. To make a Chain block, choose eight segments, two from each teal print. Sew two nonmatching segments together to make a four-patch unit. Make four units that measure 4½" square, including seam allowances.

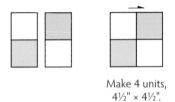

Make 4 units,
4½" × 4½".

3. Arrange the four-patch units, two white 2½" × 4½" rectangles, and one white 2½" × 10½" rectangle in three rows. Sew the pieces together into rows, and then join the rows to complete a Chain block that measures 10½" square, including seam allowances. Make 17 Chain blocks.

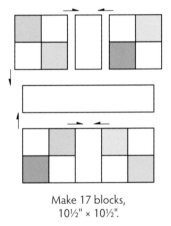

Make 17 blocks,
10½" × 10½".

assembling the quilt top

1. Referring to the quilt assembly diagram on page 37, arrange the Sister's Choice blocks and Chain blocks in seven rows of five blocks each, alternating the block designs as shown. Sew the blocks together into rows, and then join the rows. The quilt center should measure 50½" × 70½", including seam allowances.

2. For the inner border, sew the white 2" × 42" strips together end to end to make one long strip. Press the seam allowances open. Cut two strips, 2" × 70½", and sew them to opposite sides of the quilt top. Cut two strips, 2" × 53½", and sew them to the top and bottom of the quilt top.

3. For the middle border, sew the medium teal 1½" × 42" strips together end to end to make one long strip. Press the seam allowances open. Cut two strips, 1½" × 73½", and sew them to opposite sides of the quilt top. Cut two strips, 1½" × 55½", and sew them to the top and bottom of the quilt top.

4. For the outer border, sew the light teal 3½" × 42" strips together end to end to make one long strip. Press the seam allowances open. Cut two strips, 3½" × 75½", and sew them to opposite sides of the quilt top. Cut two strips, 3½" × 61½", and sew them to the top and bottom of the quilt top. The completed quilt top should measure 61½" × 81½".

finishing the quilt

For more details about any of the finishing steps, go to ShopMartingale.com/HowtoQuilt.

1. Layer the backing, batting, and quilt top; baste the layers together.

2. Quilt by hand or machine. The quilt shown is machine quilted with an allover starburst design.

3. Trim the excess batting and backing fabric from the quilt. Use the dark teal 2½"-wide strips to make double-fold binding, and then attach the binding to the quilt.

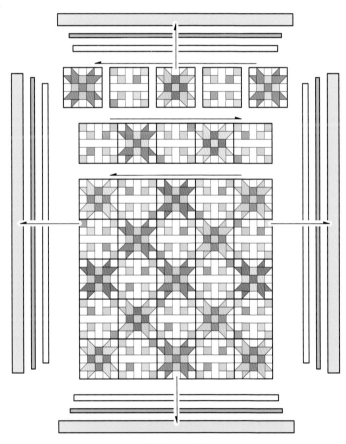

Quilt assembly

Winsome

Spring is my favorite season. Each year I look forward to tulips, daffodils, and lilacs making their first appearance and color returning to the world. As a kid I would spend afternoons in the field behind my house riding my bike, picking lilacs, and soaking in the sunshine. This quilt reminds me of those breezy spring days.

materials

Yardage is based on 42"-wide fabric. Fat quarters measure 18" × 21".

- 10 fat quarters of assorted prints for blocks
- 4⅛ yards of white solid for background, sashing, and inner and outer borders
- ⅝ yard of dark teal print for middle border
- ⅝ yard of light teal print for binding
- 5½ yards of fabric for backing
- 76" × 92" piece of batting

cutting

All measurements include ¼" seam allowances.

From *each of 8* print fat quarters, cut:

2 strips, 2¼" × 21"; crosscut into 12 rectangles, 2¼" × 3¼" (96 total)

2 strips, 6" × 21"; crosscut into 12 rectangles, 3¼" × 6" (96 total)

From *each of 2* print fat quarters, cut:

2 strips, 6" × 21"; crosscut into 8 rectangles, 3¼" × 6" (16 total)

2 strips, 2¼" × 21"; crosscut into 8 rectangles, 2¼" × 3¼" (16 total)

From the white solid, cut:

2 strips, 11½" × 42"; crosscut into:

- 23 strips, 1½" × 11½"
- 4 strips, 6½" × 11½"

10 strips, 4¼" × 42"; crosscut into 112 rectangles, 3¼" × 4¼"

8 strips, 3" × 42"

7 strips, 2" × 42"

8 strips, 2¾" × 42"; crosscut into 112 squares, 2¾" × 2¾"

5 strips, 1½" × 42"; crosscut into 112 squares, 1½" × 1½"

From the dark teal print, cut:

7 strips, 2½" × 42"

From the light teal print, cut:

8 strips, 2½" × 42"

finished quilt: 67½" × 83½"

finished block: 11" × 11"

making the blocks

Press the seam allowances as indicated by the arrows.

1. For one block, select matching 3¼" × 6" and 2¼" × 3¼" rectangles from *each* of four different prints.

Plan It Out

Before I start piecing, I like to decide which prints will be in each block. I make a stack of prints for each block—in this case it would be 28 stacks of four prints in each. This helps to guarantee a good variety of colors in each block, and I won't be stuck with four pink prints in the final block.

2. Draw a diagonal line from corner to corner on the wrong side of each white 2¾" square. Place a marked white square on the top-right corner of a print 3¼" × 6" rectangle, right sides together and with the line oriented as shown. Sew on the drawn line. Trim ¼" from the line and flip the corner up. Repeat to make four units that measure 3¼" × 6", including seam allowances.

 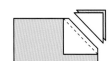

Make 4 units,
3¼" × 6".

3. Draw a diagonal line from corner to corner on the wrong side of each white 1½" square.

4. Place a marked white square on the top-right corner of a print 2¼" × 3¼" rectangle, right sides together and with the line oriented as shown. Sew on the drawn line. Trim ¼" from the line and flip the corner open. Repeat to make four units that measure 2¼" × 3¼", including seam allowances.

Make 4 units,
2¼" × 3¼".

5. Sew a white 3¼" × 4¼" rectangle to one side of each unit from step 4. Make four units that measure 3¼" × 6", including seam allowances.

 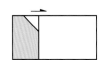

Make 4 units,
3¼" × 6".

6. Lay out the block elements to determine your desired color placement for the block. Sew a unit from step 2 to a unit from step 5 to make a quarter block that measures 6" square, including seam allowances. Make four quarter blocks.

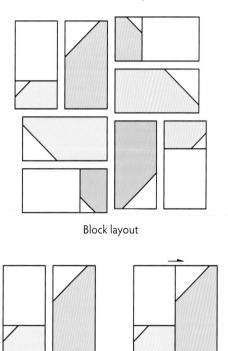

Block layout

Make 4 units,
6" × 6".

7. Arrange the quarter blocks into two rows, rotating as needed. Sew the blocks together into rows, and then join the rows to complete a block that measures 11½" square, including seam allowances. Make 28 blocks.

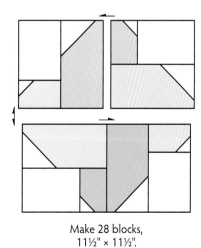

Make 28 blocks,
11½" × 11½".

assembling the quilt top

1. Refer to the quilt assembly diagram on page 43 for guidance as needed. For columns 1, 3, and 5, sew six blocks together with a white 1½" × 11½" rectangle between each block. For columns 2 and 4, sew five blocks together with a white 1½" × 11½" rectangle between each block and a white 6½" × 11½" rectangle on each end. Each column should measure 11½" × 71½", including the seam allowances. Sew the columns together. The quilt center should measure 55½" × 71½", including seam allowances.

2. For the inner border, sew the white 2" × 42" strips together end to end to make one long strip. Press the seam allowances open. Cut two strips, 2" × 71½", and sew them to opposite sides of the quilt top. Cut two strips, 2" × 58½", and sew them to the top and bottom of the quilt top. The quilt top should measure 58½" × 74½", including seam allowances.

3. For the middle border, sew the dark teal 2½" × 42" strips together end to end to make one long strip. Press the seam allowances open. Cut two strips, 2½" × 74½", and sew them to opposite sides of the quilt top. Cut two strips, 2½" × 62½", and sew them to the top and bottom of the quilt top. The quilt top should measure 62½" × 78½", including seam allowances.

4. For the outer border, sew the white 3" × 42" white strips together end to end to make one long strip. Press the seam allowances open. Cut two strips, 2½" × 78½", and sew them to opposite sides of the quilt top. Cut two strips, 2½" × 67½", and sew them to the top and bottom of the quilt top. The completed quilt top should measure 67½" × 83½".

finishing the quilt

For more details about any of the finishing steps, go to ShopMartingale.com/HowtoQuilt.

1. Layer the backing, batting, and quilt top; baste the layers together.

2. Quilt by hand or machine. The quilt shown is machine quilted with an allover flower design.

3. Trim the excess batting and backing fabric from the quilt. Use the light teal 2½"-wide strips to make double-fold binding, and then attach the binding to the quilt.

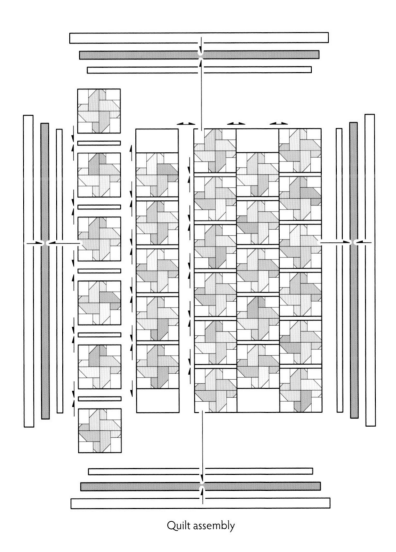

Quilt assembly

Game Night

We love getting together with friends and family for game nights. We talk, we laugh, we eat, and sometimes we even get around to actually playing board games. The shapes and colors in this quilt remind me of some of the classic board games we played as kids.

materials

Yardage is based on 42"-wide fabric. Fat quarters measure 18" × 21".

- 7 fat quarters of assorted bright prints for blocks
- 3 fat quarters of assorted black prints for appliqué circles
- 4¼ yards of white solid for background, sashing, and border
- ⅝ yard of aqua print for binding
- 4 yards of fabric for backing
- 66" × 80" piece of batting
- EZ Tri-Recs rulers or nonslip template plastic
- Perfect Circles template (optional)
- Heat-resistant Mylar template sheets (optional)
- 1⅓ yards of 17"-wide fusible web (optional)
- Basting glue
- Spray starch

• • • • • • •

finished quilt: 59" × 73"
finished block: 12" × 12"

cutting

All measurements include ¼" seam allowances. See "Triangle Cutting Tips" on page 47 before cutting the triangles.

From *1* of the bright print fat quarters, cut:
3 strips, 2½" × 21"
2 strips, 4½" × 21"; crosscut into 8 A triangles

From *each of 6* bright print fat quarters, cut:
3 strips, 2½" × 21" (18 total)
2 strips, 4½" × 21"; crosscut into 12 A triangles (72 total)

From the white solid, cut:
11 strips, 4½" × 42"; crosscut into:
  • 20 squares, 4½" × 4½"
  • 160 B triangles
1 strip, 21" × 42"; crosscut into 15 strips, 2½" × 21"
15 strips, 2½" × 42"; crosscut 9 of the strips into:
  • 6 strips, 2½" × 21"
  • 15 rectangles, 2½" × 12½"
7 strips, 2¾" × 42"

From the aqua print, cut:
7 strips, 2½" × 42"

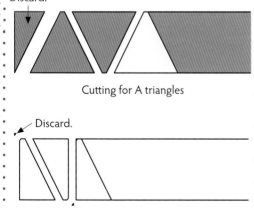
making the blocks

Press the seam allowances as indicated by the arrows.

1. Select four matching A triangles and eight B triangles. Sew B triangles to opposite sides of an A triangle to make one triangle-in-a-square unit that measures 4½" square, including seam allowances. Make four matching units. Repeat to make 20 sets of four matching triangle-in-a-square units.

Make 4 units, 4½" × 4½".

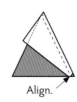
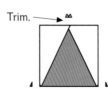

2. Sew a white and a print 2½" × 21" strip together to make a strip set. Repeat to make 21 strip sets. Cut each strip set into 2½"-wide segments for a total of 160 segments that measure 2½" × 4½", including seam allowances. Sort the segments into 20 groups of eight. Each group should have one of each print with one print repeated.

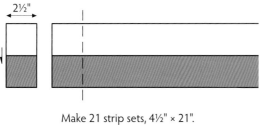

Make 21 strip sets, 4½" × 21".
Cut 160 segments, 2½" × 4½".

3. Working with just one group at a time, sew two segments together to make a four-patch unit that measures 4½" square, including seam allowances. Repeat to make four units from each group.

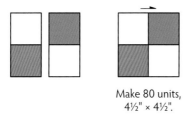

Make 80 units,
4½" × 4½".

4. Two different options for making the circles are described in this step—using a circle template and fusible appliqué. Make a circle template from a heat-resistant Mylar template sheet using the pattern on page 50 or use the 3½" Perfect Circles template. Use a pencil to trace 32 circles total onto the wrong sides of the black fat quarters. Cut out each circle, leaving a ¼" seam allowance all the way around. Using a long basting stitch, machine stitch around each circle through the center of the seam allowance, leaving the threads long as you begin and end stitching. Place the template on the wrong side of the circle and pull the bobbin threads to gather the circle around the template. Press the seam allowance with a medium-hot iron. Spray a little starch on the seam allowance as you go to create a nice, crisp edge. Remove the template, clip the threads, and press the circle once more. Repeat

to prepare 32 circles for appliqué. To use the optional fusible-appliqué method, use a pencil to trace 32 circles, 3½" diameter, onto the paper side of the fusible web. Cut out each circle about ¼" outside the traced line. Following the manufacturer's instructions, press the circles onto the wrong side of the black fat quarters. With scissors, carefully cut out each circle along the drawn line. Remove the paper backing.

5. Center one circle on a white 4½" square. Glue baste in place (or press in place if using the fusible-appliqué option). Machine stitch around the circle with a straight, blanket, or zigzag stitch and coordinating thread. Repeat to make 20 appliqué units. Save the remaining 12 circles for step 5 of "Assembling the Quilt Top."

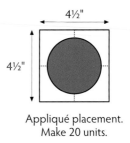

Appliqué placement.
Make 20 units.

6. Select four matching triangle-in-a-square units, one group of four-patch units from step 3, and one appliqué unit from step 5. Arrange into three rows as shown, noting the orientation of the four-patch units, and then sew into rows. Join the rows to make a block that measures 12½" square, including seam allowances. Make 20 blocks.

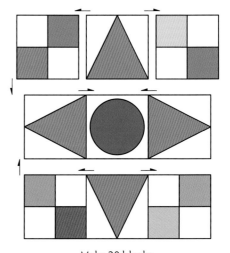

Make 20 blocks,
12½" × 12½".

assembling the quilt top

1. Sew the six white 2½" × 42" strips together end to end to make one long strip. Press the seam allowances open. From this long strip, cut four 54½"-long strips.

2. Referring to the quilt assembly diagram below, arrange the blocks into five rows of four blocks each, positioning the white 2½" × 12½" rectangles between the blocks. Add the white 54½"-long sashing strips between the rows.

3. Sew the blocks and sashing rectangles into rows, and then join the rows with the horizontal sashing strips. The quilt top should measure 54½" × 68½", including seam allowances.

4. For the border, sew the white 2¾" × 42" strips together end to end to make one long strip. Press the seam allowances open. Cut two strips, 2¾" × 68½", and sew them to opposite sides of the quilt top. Cut two strips, 2¾" × 59", and sew them to the top and bottom of the quilt top. The completed quilt top should measure 59" × 73".

5. Center the remaining 12 circles over each vertical and horizontal sashing intersection as shown in the circle placement diagram. Glue baste the circles in place (or press in place if using the fusible-appliqué option). Machine stitch around each circle as before.

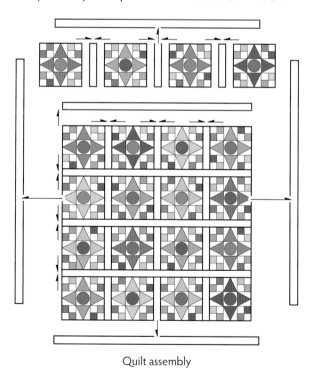

Quilt assembly

Circle placement

finishing the quilt

For more details about any of the finishing steps, go to ShopMartingale.com/HowtoQuilt.

1. Layer the backing, batting, and quilt top; baste the layers together.

2. Quilt by hand or machine. The quilt shown is machine quilted with an allover circle design.

3. Trim the excess batting and backing fabric from the quilt. Use the aqua 2½"-wide strips to make double-fold binding, and then attach the binding to the quilt.

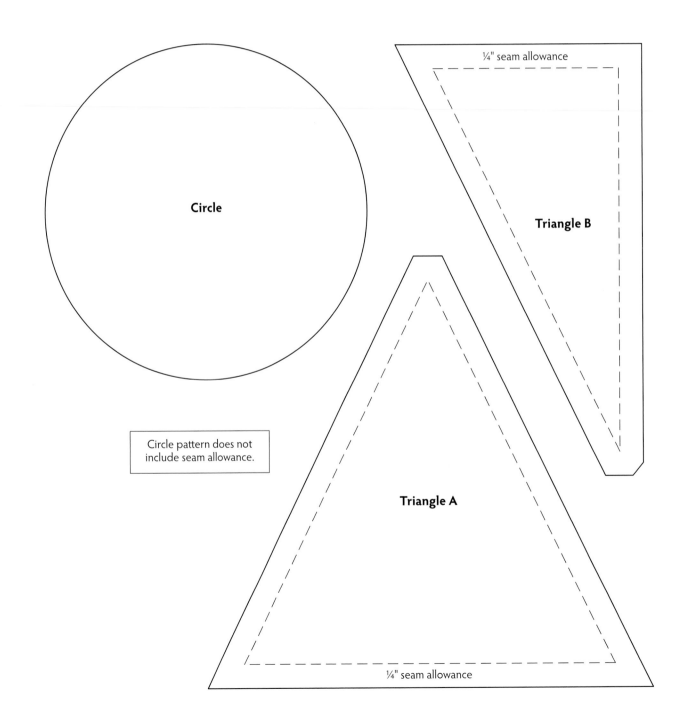

Circle

¼" seam allowance

Triangle B

Circle pattern does not include seam allowance.

Triangle A

¼" seam allowance

Stellar

It's time to pull out those fun low-volume background prints and put them to good use. To add interest to the quilt background, choose fat quarters in a range of values (light versus dark) and a mix of prints, including geometric designs, text motifs, dots, and swirls. Or you could change up the whole look of the quilt by choosing a variety of navy prints for the background and using yellow prints for the stars to really let them glow.

materials

Yardage is based on 42"-wide fabric. Fat quarters measure 18" × 21".

:: 9 fat quarters of assorted gray prints for background

:: 3 fat quarters for stars (teal, fuchsia, and yellow solids)

:: ½ yard of dark gray print for binding

:: 3 yards of fabric for backing

:: 51" × 61" piece of batting

cutting

All measurements include ¼" seam allowances.

From *each* of the 9 gray fat quarters, cut:

5 strips, 3½" × 21" (45 total); crosscut into:
  • 6 rectangles, 3½" × 10" (54 total)
  • 4 rectangles, 3½" × 5¼" (36 total)
  • 4 rectangles, 2" × 3½" (36 total)
  • 4 squares, 2" × 2" (36 total)

From *each* of the teal, fuchsia, and yellow fat quarters, cut:

3 strips, 2" × 21"; crosscut into 24 squares, 2" × 2" (72 total)

1 strip, 3½" × 21"; crosscut into 3 squares, 3½" × 3½" (9 total)

From the dark gray print, cut:

6 strips, 2½" × 42"

finished quilt: 44½" × 54½"
finished block: 6" × 6"

making the blocks

Press the seam allowances as indicated by the arrows.

1. Draw a diagonal line from corner to corner on the wrong side of eight teal 2" squares.

2. Place a marked teal square on one end of a gray 2" × 3½" rectangle, right sides together and with the line oriented as shown. Sew on the drawn line. Trim ¼" from the line and flip the corner open. Repeat to sew a marked teal square to the other end of the gray rectangle as shown to complete one star-point unit. Make four matching star-point units that measure 2" × 3½", including seam allowances.

Make 4 units,
2" × 3½".

3. Arrange four star-point units, one teal 3½" square, and four matching gray 2" squares in three rows as shown. Sew the pieces together into rows, and then join the rows to make a Sawtooth Star block that measures 6½" square, including seam allowances. Make nine blocks total, three each from teal, fuchsia, and yellow.

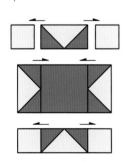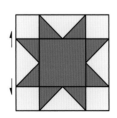

Make 9 blocks,
6½" × 6½".

assembling the quilt top

1. This quilt is made up of nine rows. Each row will use one Sawtooth Star block, six large (3½" × 10") bricks, and four small (3½" × 5¼") bricks.

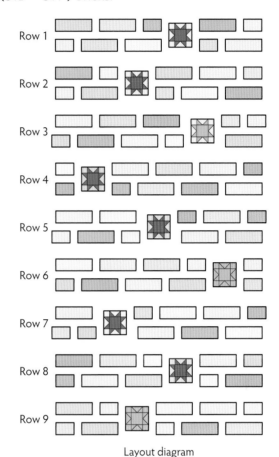

Layout diagram

Lay It Out

It helps to arrange the entire quilt on a design wall or flat surface before sewing. Once all the pieces are laid out, check to make sure the darkest and lightest background prints are evenly spread throughout the quilt. Because there are only two brick sizes, it's easy to swap one brick for a different one of the same size until you're happy with the layout.

2. Arrange the bricks and blocks in each row as shown in the assembly diagram. Each numbered row is made up of four partial rows (A, B, C, and D) on either side of the stars. Sew each partial row together first. Then sew row A to row B, and row C to row D. Sew together with a Sawtooth Star block to make a row measuring 6½" × 44½", including seam allowances.

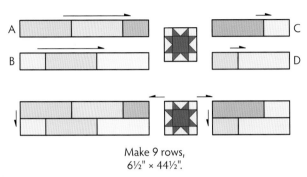

Make 9 rows,
6½" × 44½".

3. Assemble all the rows, and then sew the rows together. The completed quilt top should measure 44½" × 54½".

finishing the quilt

For more details about any of the finishing steps, go to ShopMartingale.com/HowtoQuilt.

1. Layer the backing, batting, and quilt top; baste the layers together.

2. Quilt by hand or machine. The quilt shown is machine quilted with horizontal wavy lines.

3. Trim the excess batting and backing fabric from the quilt. Use the dark gray 2½"-wide strips to make double-fold binding, and then attach the binding to the quilt.

Quilt assembly

Sunny Day

fat quarters 12

Each week my family gave a sweet older woman a ride to church. And every week without fail, no matter the weather, this pleasant woman would say, "Isn't it a *beautiful* day?" In my eight-year-old opinion, only the sunny days were the beautiful ones. I've since learned to find the beauty in even stormy skies. This Sunny Day quilt is a reminder that each day is beautiful.

materials

Yardage is based on 42"-wide fabric. Fat quarters measure 18" x 21".

- 5 fat quarters of assorted pink prints for blocks
- 7 fat quarters of assorted yellow prints for blocks
- 2⅝ yards of white solid for background and borders
- 2 yards of green print for sashing and scallop border
- ⅝ yard of pink print for binding
- 5⅛ yards of fabric for backing
- 71" × 85" piece of batting

finished quilt: 63" × 77"

finished block: 12" × 12"

cutting

All measurements include ¼" seam allowances.

From *each* of the 5 pink print fat quarters, cut:

2 strips, 4" × 21"; crosscut into 8 squares, 4" × 4" (40 total)

2 strips, 3½" × 21"; crosscut into 16 rectangles, 2" × 3½" (80 total)

From *each* of the 7 yellow print fat quarters, cut:

2 strips, 4" × 21"; crosscut into 6 squares, 4" × 4" (42 total; 2 will be extra)

2 strips, 3½" × 21"; crosscut into 12 squares, 3½" × 3½" (84 total; 4 will be extra)

From the white solid, cut:

2 strips, 3½" × 42"; crosscut into 20 squares, 3½" × 3½"

26 strips, 2" × 42"; crosscut into:
- 80 rectangles, 2" × 3½"
- 80 rectangles, 2" × 5"
- 160 squares, 2" × 2"

5 strips, 1½" × 42"; crosscut into 108 squares, 1½" × 1½"

1 strip, 3¼" × 42"; crosscut into 4 squares, 3¼" × 3¼"

7 strips, 2" × 42"

Continued on page 58

Continued from page 57

From the green print, cut:

1 strip, 12½" × 42"; crosscut into 15 rectangles, 2½" × 12½"

4 strips, 2" × 42"; crosscut into 80 squares, 2" × 2"

8 strips, 3¼" × 42"; crosscut into:
- 50 rectangles, 3¼" × 5"
- 4 rectangles, 3¼" × 5¼"

6 strips, 2½" × 42"

From the pink print yardage, cut:

8 strips, 2½" × 42"

Blocks That Shine

The center of each Sunshine block features two yellow prints. To make the blocks really shine, select yellows with different values—one light print and one dark. If the yellows are too close in value, they will blend together within the block.

making the blocks

Press the seam allowances as indicated by the arrows.

1. Draw a diagonal line from corner to corner on the wrong side of two matching yellow 4" squares. Place a marked yellow square on a pink 4" square, right sides together. Sew ¼" from each side of the drawn line. Cut along the drawn line to make two half-square-triangle units. Trim the units to measure 3½" square, including seam allowances. Make four matching units.

Make 4 units.

2. Sew a white 2" × 3½" rectangle to one side of a half-square-triangle unit, noting the orientation of the half-square-triangle unit. Sew a white 2" × 5" rectangle to the adjacent side of the half-square-triangle unit. Make four units that measure 5" square, including seam allowances.

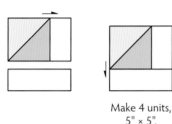

Make 4 units, 5" × 5".

3. Draw a diagonal line from corner to corner on the wrong side of four green 2" squares. Place a marked square on one corner of the unit from step 3, right sides together and with the line oriented as shown. Sew on the drawn line. Trim ¼" from the line and flip the corner open. Repeat to make four corner units that measure 5" square, including seam allowances.

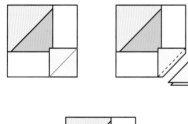

Make 4 units, 5" × 5".

4. Draw a diagonal line from corner to corner on the wrong side of eight white 2" squares. Place a marked square on one end of a pink 2" × 3½" rectangle, right sides together, with the line oriented as shown. Sew on the line. Trim ¼" from the line and flip the corner open. Repeat to sew a marked white square to the other end of the pink rectangle as shown to complete one

flying-geese unit. Make four matching units that measure 2" × 3½", including seam allowances.

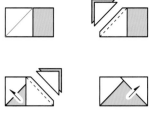

Make 4 units,
2" × 3½".

5. Sew a yellow 3½" square (different from the yellow used in step 1) to the bottom of a flying-geese unit. Make four matching units that measure 3½" × 5", including seam allowances.

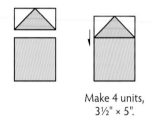

Make 4 units,
3½" × 5".

6. Arrange four corner units, four units from step 5, and one white 3½" square into three rows. Sew the pieces into rows, and then join the rows to make a block that measures 12½" square, including seam allowances. Make 20 blocks.

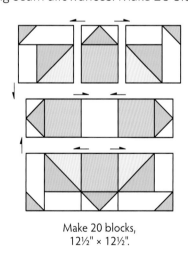

Make 20 blocks,
12½" × 12½".

assembling the quilt top

1. Join the green 2½" × 42" strips end to end to make one long strip. Press seam allowances open. From this strip, cut four strips, 2½" × 54½".

2. Referring to the quilt assembly diagram on page 61, arrange the blocks into five rows of four blocks each, positioning the green 2½" × 12½" sashing rectangles between the blocks. Add the green 54½"-long strips between the rows.

3. Sew the blocks and sashing rectangles into rows, and then sew the rows to the horizontal sashing strips. The quilt top should measure 54½" × 68½", including seam allowances.

4. Draw a diagonal line from corner to corner on the wrong side of each white 1½" square. Place a marked square on the top-left corner of a green 3¼" × 5" rectangle, right sides together and with the line oriented as shown. Sew on the line. Trim ¼" from the line and flip the corner open. Repeat to sew a marked square to the top-right corner of the green rectangle as shown. Repeat to make 50 scallop units, 3¼" × 5", and four units, 3¼" × 5¼".

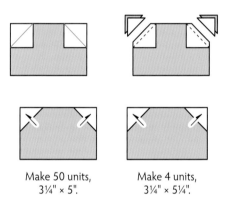

Make 50 units,
3¼" × 5".

Make 4 units,
3¼" × 5¼".

Playing Tricks

For the side borders to fit, two scallops need to be slightly longer than the others. Adding just ¼" to two scallops makes the math work, but the difference isn't noticeable in the finished quilt. Just be sure you add two of the longer (3¼" × 5¼") scallop blocks to each side border.

5. Join 13 of the 3¼" × 5" scallop units and sew a 3¼" × 5¼" unit to each end. Make two side borders that measure 3¼" × 68½", including seam allowances. Sew the borders to opposite sides of the quilt top.

Make 2 side borders,
3¼" × 68½".

6. Join 12 of the 3¼" × 5" scallop units and sew a white 3¼" square to each end. Make two borders that measure 3¼" × 60", including seam allowances. Sew these borders to the top and bottom of the quilt top.

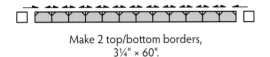

Make 2 top/bottom borders,
3¼" × 60".

7. For the outer border, sew the white 2" × 42" strips together end to end to make one long strip. Press the seam allowances open. Cut two strips, 2" × 74", and sew them to opposite sides of the quilt top. Cut two strips, 2" × 63", and sew them to the top and bottom of the quilt top. The completed quilt top should measure 63" × 77".

finishing the quilt

For more details about any of the finishing steps, go to ShopMartingale.com/HowtoQuilt.

1. Layer the backing, batting, and quilt top; baste the layers together.

2. Quilt by hand or machine. The quilt shown is machine quilted with an allover design of swirls and leaves.

3. Trim the excess batting and backing fabric from the quilt. Use the pink 2½"-wide strips to make double-fold binding, and then attach the binding to the quilt.

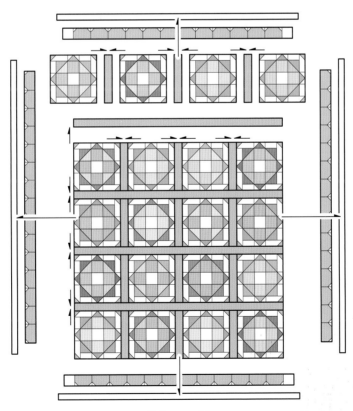

Quilt assembly

Grandstand

A tricky-looking quilt that's not tricky to piece—that's Grandstand. This quilt has five different blocks but an endless number of ways to arrange them; each quilt will be unique. And the size of these blocks makes them perfect for using your favorite medium- and large-scale prints.

fat quarters 14

materials

Yardage is based on 42"-wide fabric. Fat quarters measure 18" × 21".

- 14 fat quarters of assorted prints for blocks
- 3⅝ yards of white solid for background, sashing, and border
- ¾ yard of aqua print for binding
- 7⅝ yards of fabric for backing
- 85" × 96" piece of batting

cutting

All measurements include ¼" seam allowances.

From *each* of the 14 print fat quarters, cut:

1 strip, 10½" × 21"; crosscut into 4 rectangles, 5" × 10½" (56 total; 1 will be extra)

1 strip, 5" × 21"; crosscut into 4 squares, 5" × 5" (56 total; 1 will be extra)

From the white solid, cut:

3 strips, 6" × 42"; crosscut into 20 rectangles, 5" × 6"

2 strips, 10½" × 42"; crosscut into:
- 5 rectangles, 6" × 10½"
- 25 rectangles, 1½" × 10½"

5 strips, 1½" × 42"; crosscut into 35 rectangles, 1½" × 5"

2 strips, 16" × 42"; crosscut into 45 rectangles, 1½" × 16"

8 strips, 1½" × 42"

8 strips, 3¼" × 42"

From the aqua print, cut:

9 strips, 2½" × 42"

* * * * * * *

finished quilt: 76½" x 87½"

finished block: 15½" x 15½" and 4½" x 15½"

making the blocks

Press the seam allowances as indicated by the arrows.

A BLOCKS

1. Select three print squares, two print rectangles, one white 6" × 10½" rectangle, two white 1½" × 5" rectangles, one white 1½" × 10½" rectangle, and one white 1½" × 16" rectangle.

2. Sew print squares to opposite sides of a white 1½" × 5" rectangle. Sew a white 6" × 10½" rectangle to the bottom.

3. Sew a white 1½" × 10½" rectangle and a print rectangle to the unit from step 2.

4. Sew a print square and a print rectangle to opposite sides of a white 1½" × 5" rectangle. Then sew this unit and the unit from step 3 to opposite sides of a white 1½" × 16" rectangle to complete a block that measures 16" square, including seam allowances. Repeat to make five of block A.

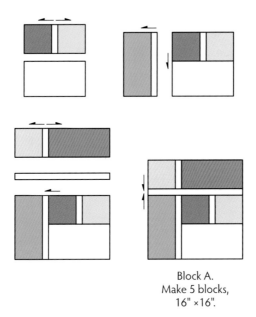

Block A.
Make 5 blocks,
16" × 16".

Leave It to Chance

There are two ways to approach this quilt. Lay it all out on a design wall or floor space, or leave it to chance! For the unplanned approach, place all of the print squares in one bag and the print rectangles in another. Pull pieces randomly as you go. Then when you're arranging your quilt top you can swap blocks and rotate them until you're happy with the layout.

B BLOCKS

1. Select three print rectangles, one print square, two white 5" × 6" rectangles, one white 1½" × 5" rectangle, and two white 1½" × 16" rectangles.

2. Arrange the block elements as shown. Sew together into rows, and then join the rows and the white 1½" × 16" rectangles in alternating positions to complete a block that measures 16" square, including seam allowances. Repeat to make five of block B.

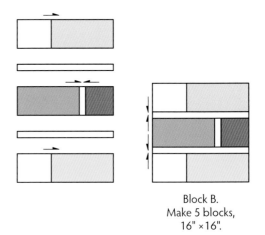

Block B.
Make 5 blocks,
16" × 16".

C BLOCKS

1. Select two print squares, three print rectangles, one white 5" × 6" rectangle, one white 1½" × 5" rectangle, two white 1½" × 10½" rectangles, and one white 1½" × 16" rectangle.

2. Sew a print square to the white 5" × 6" rectangle. Sew this unit and a print rectangle to opposite sides of a white 1½" × 10½" rectangle.

3. Sew a white 1½" × 10½" rectangle and a print rectangle to the unit from step 2.

4. Sew a print square and a print rectangle to opposite sides of a white 1½" × 5" rectangle. Then sew this unit and the unit from step 3 to opposite sides of a white 1½" × 16" rectangle to complete a block that measures 16" square, including seam allowances. Repeat to make five of block C.

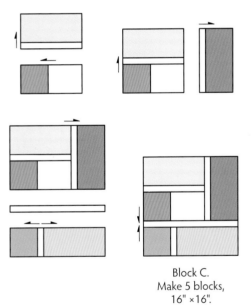

Block C.
Make 5 blocks,
16" ×16".

D BLOCKS

1. Select two print squares, three print rectangles, one white 5" × 6" rectangle, one white 1½" × 5" rectangle, two white 1½" × 10½" rectangles, and one white 1½" × 16" rectangle.

2. Sew a print square to the white 5" × 6" rectangle. Then sew this unit and a print rectangle to opposite sides of a white 1½" × 10½" rectangle.

3. Sew a white 1½" × 10½" rectangle and a print rectangle to the unit from step 2.

4. Sew a print square and a print rectangle to opposite sides of a white 1½" × 5" rectangle. Then sew this unit and the unit from step 3 to opposite sides of a white 1½" × 16" rectangle to complete a block that measures 16" square, including seam allowances. Repeat to make five of block D.

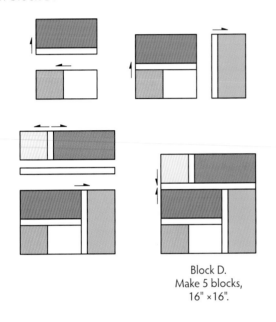

Block D.
Make 5 blocks,
16" ×16".

E BLOCKS

Sew three print squares and two white 1½" × 5" rectangles together as shown to complete a block that measures 5" × 16", including seam allowances. Repeat to make five of block E.

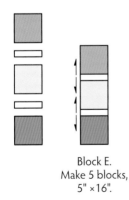

Block E.
Make 5 blocks,
5" ×16".

assembling the quilt top

1. Arrange the blocks into five rows of five blocks each. Each row should have four large blocks (A, B, C, or D) and one small block (E). The diagram below is a suggested layout (see "Mix and Match" below). Place white 1½" × 16" sashing rectangles between all blocks.

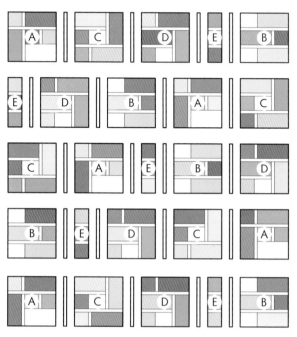

Layout diagram

Mix and Match

As long as each row contains four big blocks (A, B, C, or D) and one small block (E), you can swap blocks, rotate them, and move them around as much as you want! There's no one "right" way to arrange the blocks. Think of it as a puzzle with many, many solutions.

2. Sew the blocks and sashing rectangles together into rows.

Make 5 rows,
16" × 71".

3. Sew the white 1½" × 42" strips together end to end to make one long strip. Press the seam allowances open. From this long strip, cut four strips, 1½" × 71".

4. Join the rows, alternating them with the 71"-long sashing strips. As you join the rows, watch for points where the vertical sashing from one row needs to line up with the vertical sashing in the next row. Pin at these intersections to make sure the rows don't shift as you sew them together with the horizontal sashing strips. The quilt top should measure 71" × 82", including seam allowances.

5. For the border, sew the white 3¼" × 42" strips together end to end to make one long strip. Press the seam allowances open. Cut two strips, 3¼" × 82", and sew them to opposite sides of the quilt top. Cut two strips, 3¼" × 76½", and sew them to the top and bottom. The completed quilt top should measure 76½" × 87½".

finishing the quilt

For more details about any of the finishing steps, go to ShopMartingale.com/HowtoQuilt.

1. Layer the backing, batting, and quilt top; baste the layers together.

2. Quilt by hand or machine. The quilt shown is machine quilted with an allover circle design.

3. Trim the excess batting and backing fabric from the quilt. Use the aqua 2½"-wide strips to make double-fold binding, and then attach the binding to the quilt.

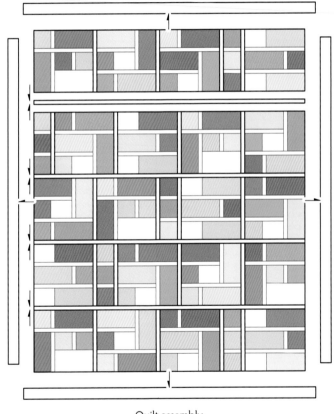

Quilt assembly

Venture Out

When I first got my driver's license as a teenager, I was terribly nervous to drive downtown because of all the one-way streets. To this day I still have a fear of driving the wrong way on a one-way street, but (thank goodness) it's never happened … yet. In this quilt, each column is like a one-way road—all of the arrows point in one direction, and the seam allowances for each column are pressed in the same direction as the arrows.

materials

Yardage is based on 42"-wide fabric. Fat quarters measure 18" × 21".

:: 14 fat quarters of assorted prints for blocks

:: 4⅔ yards of white dot for background, sashing, and border

:: ⅝ yard of aqua print for binding

:: 5¼ yards of fabric for backing

:: 72" × 88" piece of batting

• • • • • • •

finished quilt: 64" × 80"

finished block: 4" × 12½"

cutting

All measurements include ¼" seam allowances.

From *each of 10* print fat quarters, cut:

1 strip, 7" × 21"; crosscut into 4 rectangles, 4½" × 7" (40 total)

2 strips, 4½" × 21"; crosscut into:
  • 1 rectangle, 4½" × 7" (10 total)
  • 10 rectangles, 2½" × 4½" (100 total)

From *each of 4* print fat quarters, cut:

1 strip, 7" × 21"; crosscut into 4 rectangles, 4½" × 7" (16 total)

1 strip, 4½" × 21"; crosscut into 8 rectangles, 2½" × 4½" (32 total)

From the white dot, cut:

17 strips, 1½" × 42"; crosscut into 132 rectangles, 1½" × 4½"

27 strips, 2½" × 42"; crosscut into 396 squares, 2½" × 2½"

19 strips, 2" × 42"

7 strips, 2¾" × 42"

From the aqua print, cut:

8 strips, 2½" × 42"

making the blocks

Press the seam allowances as indicated by the arrows.

1. Draw a diagonal line from corner to corner on the wrong side of each white dot 2½" square.

2. Place a marked white square on one end of a print 2½" × 4½" rectangle, right sides together and with the line oriented as shown. Sew on the drawn line. Trim ¼" from the line and flip the corner open. Repeat to sew a marked white square to the other end of the print rectangle as shown to make one flying-geese unit. Make 132 units that measure 2½" × 4½", including seam allowances.

Make 132 units,
2½" × 4½".

3. Place a marked white square on one corner of a print 4½" × 7" rectangle, right sides together and with the line oriented as shown. Sew on the drawn line. Trim ¼" from the line and flip the corner open. Repeat to sew a white square to the adjacent corner of the print rectangle to make a unit that measures 4½" × 7", including seam allowances. Make 66 units.

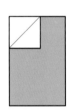 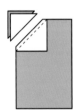
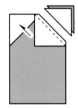 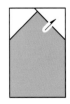

Make 66 units,
4½" × 7".

4. For one block, choose two matching flying-geese units, a matching unit from step 3, and two white 1½" × 4½" rectangles. Sew together as shown. Repeat to make 66 blocks that measure 4½" × 13", including seam allowances.

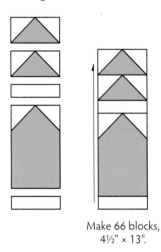

Make 66 blocks,
4½" × 13".

assembling the quilt top

1. Arrange the blocks into 11 columns of six blocks each, alternating the direction of the blocks for each column. Sew the blocks together into columns.

2. Sew the white 2" × 42" strips together end to end to make one long strip. Press the seam allowances open. Cut 10 strips, 2" × 75½", to use for vertical sashing.

Stop the Shift

To keep the columns from shifting as you join them to the sashing strips, find the center point of each column and strip, and place a pin there. Then match the center points and pin the two together all along the length of the strips. Sewing the columns together in alternating directions will help prevent shifting as well.

3. Sew the columns together, alternating them with the vertical sashing strips. The quilt top should measure 59½" × 75½", including seam allowances.

4. For the border, sew the white 2¾" × 42" strips together end to end to make one long strip. Press the seam allowances open. Cut two strips, 2¾" × 75½", and sew them to opposite sides of the quilt top. Cut two strips, 2¾" × 64", and sew them to the top and bottom of the quilt top. The completed quilt top should measure 64" × 80".

finishing the quilt

For more details about any of the finishing steps, go to ShopMartingale.com/HowtoQuilt.

1. Layer the backing, batting, and quilt top; baste the layers together.

2. Quilt by hand or machine. The quilt shown is machine quilted with an allover hexagon design.

3. Trim the excess batting and backing fabric from the quilt. Use the aqua 2½"-wide strips to make double-fold binding, and then attach the binding to the quilt.

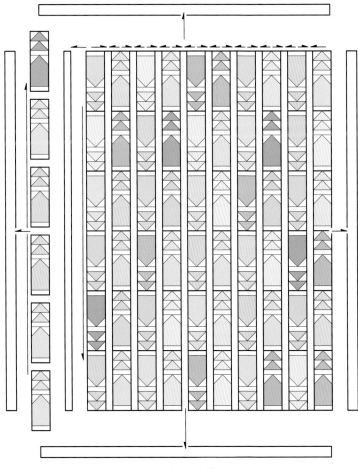

Quilt assembly

Pacific

I love having quilts that remind me of fun places, people, and memories. Years ago, we had the chance to leave our home in Utah and move to San Diego, California, for a year. We knew we would be there for just a short time, so we looked at it like an adventure. We went everywhere, saw everything, and took thousands of photos. The colors in this quilt will always remind me of our time in San Diego—the colors found at the beaches, at the parks and gardens, in the sunsets, and, yes, even the gray of those misty mornings in May.

materials

Yardage is based on 42"-wide fabric. Fat quarters measure 18" × 21".

- 14 fat quarters of assorted prints for blocks and border
- 6¼ yards of gray solid for background and border
- 1 yard of white solid for chain blocks
- ⅞ yard of navy print for binding
- 9 yards of fabric for backing
- 101" × 101" piece of batting

• • • • • • •

finished quilt: 93" x 93"
finished block: 12½" x 12½"

cutting

All measurements include ¼" seam allowances.

From *each of 3* print fat quarters, cut:

2 strips, 3" × 21"; crosscut into 11 squares, 3" × 3" (33 total; 1 will be extra)

1 strip, 5⅞" × 21"; crosscut into 2 squares, 5⅞" × 5⅞". Cut each square in half diagonally to make 2 triangles (12 total).

From *each of 11* print fat quarters, cut:

1 strip, 6" × 21"; crosscut into:

- 1 square, 5⅞" × 5⅞". Cut each square in half diagonally to make 2 triangles (22 total).
- 8 squares, 3" × 3" (88 total)

1 strip, 3" × 21"; crosscut into 4 squares, 3" × 3" (44 total)

1 strip, 5⅞" × 21"; crosscut into 3 squares, 5⅞" × 5⅞". Cut each square in half diagonally to make 2 triangles (66 total).

Continued on page 76

Continued from page 75

From the gray solid, cut:

14 strips, 3" × 42"; crosscut 6 of the strips into:

- 50 squares, 3" × 3"
- 2 rectangles, 3" × 13"
- 2 rectangles, 3" × 15½"

9 strips, 8" × 42"; crosscut into:

- 25 rectangles, 3" × 8"
- 48 rectangles, 5½" × 8"

5 strips, 3⅜" × 42"; crosscut into 50 squares, 3⅜" × 3⅜". Cut each square in half diagonally to make 100 small gray triangles.

5 strips, 5⅞" × 42" crosscut into 25 squares, 5⅞" × 5⅞". Cut each square in half diagonally to make 50 large gray triangles.

4 strips, 5½" × 42"

2 strips, 10½" × 42"; crosscut into 24 rectangles, 3" × 10½"

From the white solid, cut:

11 strips, 3" × 42"; crosscut *1* of the strips into 12 squares, 3" × 3"

From the navy print, cut:

10 strips, 2½" × 42"

Dive Right In

Don't be intimidated by the ⅜" and ⅞" measurements in the cutting directions. Making a few careful cuts in the beginning saves time in the end. Take your time and make accurate cuts, and your blocks will be beautiful.

---

making the blocks

Press the seam allowances as indicated by the arrows.

A BLOCKS

Use one print per block.

1. Sew two small gray triangles to adjacent sides of a print 3" square. Sew a matching print triangle to the pieced triangle. Make two pieced triangle units that measure 5½" square, including seam allowances.

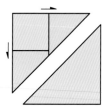

Make 2 units,
5½" × 5½".

2. Sew a print triangle and a large gray triangle together. Make two half-square-triangle units that measure 5½" square, including seam allowances.

Make 2 units,
5½" × 5½".

3. Sew a matching print 3" square to a gray 3" square. Make two units that measure 3" × 5½", including seam allowances.

Make 2 units,
3" × 5½".

4. Arrange two pieced triangle units, two half-square-triangle units, the two units from step 3, two print 3" squares, and a gray 3" × 8" rectangle into three rows as shown. Sew the pieces together into rows, and then join the rows to complete a block that measures 13" square, including seam allowances. Make 25 of block A.

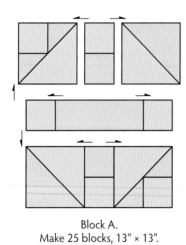

Block A.
Make 25 blocks, 13" × 13".

B BLOCKS

1. Sew gray 5½" × 42" strips to opposite sides of a white 3" × 42" strip to make a strip set that measures 13" × 42". Repeat to make two strip sets. Cut each strip set into 12 segments, 3" × 13", for a total of 24 segments.

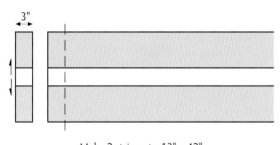

Make 2 strip sets, 13" × 42".
Cut 24 segments, 3" × 13".

Strip-Piecing Pointers

For accurate strip piecing, see my list of tips on page 15.

2. Sew a gray 3" × 42" strip and a white 3" × 42" strip together to make a strip set. Repeat to make eight strip sets. Cut each strip set into 12 segments, 3" wide, for a total of 96 segments measuring 3" × 5½", including seam allowances.

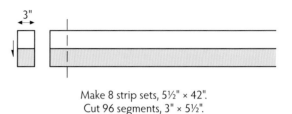

Make 8 strip sets, 5½" × 42".
Cut 96 segments, 3" × 5½".

3. Sew together two segments from step 2 to make a four-patch unit. Repeat to make 48 units that measure 5½" square, including seam allowances.

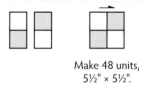

Make 48 units,
5½" × 5½".

4. Sew a gray 5½" × 8" rectangle to a four-patch unit to make a side unit, orienting the four-patch unit as shown with a white square in the top-left corner. Make 48 side units that measure 5½" × 13", including seam allowances.

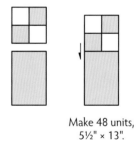

Make 48 units,
5½" × 13".

5. Arrange two side units from step 4 and a segment from step 1 as shown. Join the pieces to complete a block that measures 13" square, including seam allowances. Make 24 of block B.

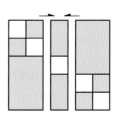

Block B.
Make 24 blocks, 13" × 13".

assembling the quilt top

1. Arrange the A blocks and B blocks in seven rows of seven blocks each, alternating the block designs as shown in the quilt assembly diagram below.

2. Sew the blocks together into rows, and then join the rows. The quilt center should measure 88" square, including seam allowances.

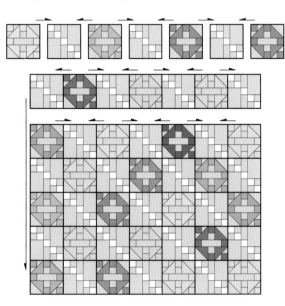

Quilt assembly

3. To make the side borders, sew three print 3" squares, three white 3" squares, six gray 3" × 10½" rectangles, and one gray 3" × 13" rectangle together as shown. Make two. The border strips should measure 3" × 88", including seam allowances. Sew the side borders to opposite sides of the quilt top, positioning the left border so that the longest gray rectangle (3" × 13") is on the bottom, and the right border so that the longest gray rectangle is at the top.

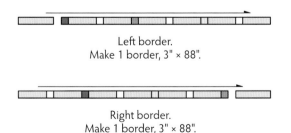

Left border.
Make 1 border, 3" × 88".

Right border.
Make 1 border, 3" × 88".

4. To make the top and bottom borders, sew four print 3" squares, three white 3" squares, six gray 3" × 10½" rectangles, and one gray 3" × 15½" rectangle together as shown. Make two. The border strips should measure 3" × 93", including seam allowances. Sew the top and bottom borders to the quilt, positioning the top border so that the longest gray rectangle (3" × 15½") is on the right end, and the bottom border so that the longest gray rectangle is on the left. The completed quilt top should measure 93" square.

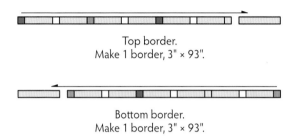

Top border.
Make 1 border, 3" × 93".

Bottom border.
Make 1 border, 3" × 93".

5. To secure the seams of the pieced border, stitch around the outside of the completed quilt top using a ⅛" seam allowance.

finishing the quilt

For more details about any of the finishing steps, go to ShopMartingale.com/HowtoQuilt.

1. Layer the backing, batting, and quilt top; baste the layers together.

2. Quilt by hand or machine. The quilt shown is machine quilted in an allover loop design.

3. Trim the excess batting and backing fabric from the quilt. Use the navy 2½"-wide strips to make double-fold binding, and then attach the binding to the quilt.

Acknowledgments

special thanks to:

Gavan, Mercer, and Finn for your hugs, words of wisdom, and encouragement, and for always saying "Yes!" when I ask, "Will you hold this quilt so I can take a photo?"

My sew-day friends for being the best cheerleaders, support group, and Viking River Cruise companions a girl could ask for.

Grandma J for handing me my first quilting needle and thread, and to **Grandma C** for being as excited as I was when I brought new fabric home from the store.

Mom and Dad for teaching me to work hard, be kind, and serve others. I want to be just like you when I grow up.

Peg for your friendship and your flawless hand-binding skills.

About the Author

Andy Knowlton has always loved color, fabric, and math, and she was delighted to discover that quilting and pattern design let her blend all three loves into one. Most afternoons you can find her in a quiet corner of her home that gets lovely, warm afternoon sunshine. It's her happy place and the inspiration for the name of her pattern company, A Bright Corner.

When Andy isn't quilting, you can find her hiking in the mountains with her dog, napping on the couch, or baking something chocolaty in her kitchen.

She lives with her husband and two kids in Utah, where they enjoy camping, exploring, playing video games, and eating cookies.

Visit Andy online at ABrightCorner.com and on Instagram at @abrightcorner.